To our parents—Bob, Anne, Brenda, and Kevin—
who instilled in us a love for the Bible and first
introduced us to God's faithful friends.

ZONDERKIDZ

Faithful Friends
Copyright © 2023 by Michael S. Kelleher and Marcy Kelleher

Requests for information should be addressed to:
Zonderkidz, *3900 Sparks Dr. SE, Grand Rapids, Michigan 49546*

ISBN 978-0-310-14355-0 (hardcover)
ISBN 978-0-310-14368-0 (audio)
ISBN 978-0-310-14366-6 (ebook)

Library of Congress Cataloging-in-Publication Data

Published in association with The Bindery Agency, www.TheBinderyAgency.com.

Zonderkidz is a trademark of Zondervan.

Zondervan titles may be purchased in bulk for educational, business, fundraising, or sales promotional use. For information, please email SpecialMarkets@Zondervan.com.

Cover Design: Cindy Davis
Photography: Marcy Kelleher
Interior Design: Denise Froehlich
Editorial: Katherine Jacobs & Mary Hassinger

Printed in China

23 24 25 26 27 DCP 10 9 8 7 6 5 4 3 2 1

faithful friends

FAVORITE STORIES
OF PEOPLE IN THE BIBLE

MICHAEL & MARCY KELLEHER

ZONDERkidz

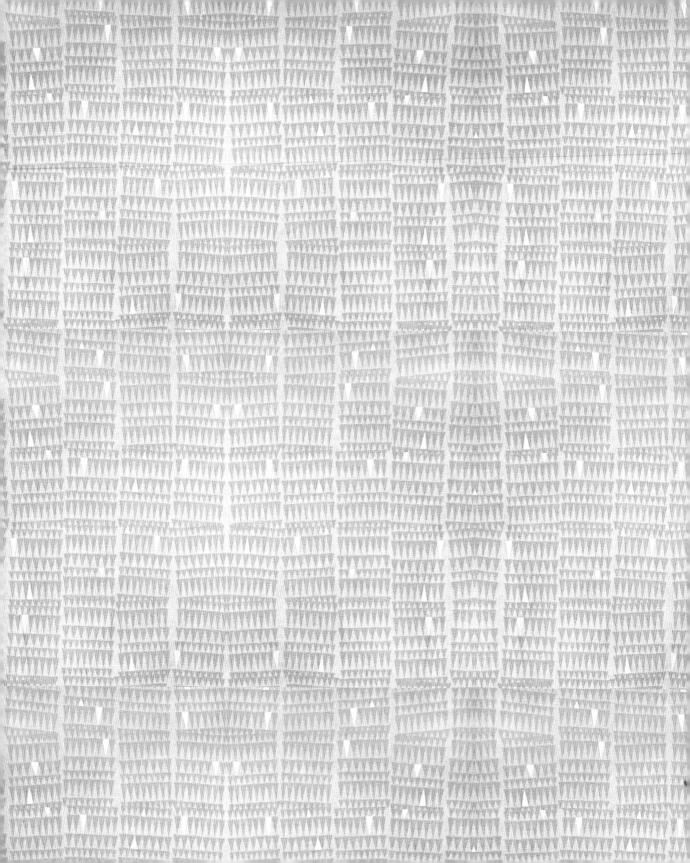

Contents

Adam and Eve

GENESIS 1–2:4

God created mankind in his own image . . .
male and female he created them.

GENESIS 1:27 (NIV)

In the beginning, God made heaven and earth, and He made light and darkness, and the sky and sea, and all the water and all the land. He made the sun and moon, the twinkling stars, and all the plants and animals. He made the birds that fly and the fish that swim, and anything that hops or gallops, scurries or slithers, creeps, crawls, prances, or prowls—anything that moves and breathes.

God looked at all He had made, and it was good. But something was missing. Or rather *someone*. Even though there were all kinds of beautiful and wonderful things, there were no people. There was no one for God to talk to. No one to love and be loved by in return. No one like Him.

So God made people. The first man and the first woman, Adam and Eve, the father and mother of everyone. He made them and put them in the garden to care for His plants and animals and to care for each other. And when He looked again at all He had made, He knew it was not just good: it was *very* good. Now there was someone like Him that He could share His love with.

Abel and Cain

GENESIS 4:1–17; HEBREWS 11:4

 By faith Abel still speaks, even though he is dead.
HEBREWS 11:4 (NIV)

Abel and Cain were the first two sons. Cain was older, but Abel was obedient to God. When they were still boys, their parents, Adam and Eve, taught them how to worship God and give thanks. The best way to do this was to give the very best they had back to God.

When they got older, the time came for Abel and Cain to bring their own offerings to God. Abel was a shepherd so he brought one of his most prized sheep: a firstborn lamb with spotless, snow-white wool. But Cain was a farmer and he brought some food he had grown. They weren't the first fruits of his harvest and not his very best, just some leftovers he didn't need anyway.

God was happy with Abel's gift but not Cain's. Cain became very jealous and angry. Why should God prefer his brother's offering over his? He became angrier and angrier until he hated his brother so much he wanted him dead.

One day Cain invited Abel out to his fields. When they were all alone, Cain suddenly attacked his brother and killed him. No one was around to see—but God saw.

"Cain, where is your brother?" God called.

Cain lied. He said he didn't know.

God answered, "His blood cries out to me from the ground."

Still Cain didn't tell the truth or say he was sorry.

In the end, God sent him away. Cain had to wander from place to place with nowhere to call home and never saw his father and mother again.

Cain's sin stuck to him like a stain. Anger and envy destroyed his soul. But Abel believed and obeyed God and God honored him for it. Because he died doing what God wanted, his example of faithfulness lives on.

Noah

 Noah was a righteous man.

GENESIS 6:9 (NIV)

The Lord told Noah He was going to send a great flood that would wash the whole world clean, but He wanted Noah and his family to be safe. So God told Noah to build an ark. It would be the biggest boat Noah had ever seen. It had to be big enough for Noah, his family, and two of every kind of animal from around the world.

Noah and his family worked on the ark for years. They worked day and night. When at last the boat was finished, God told Noah to lead his family inside. But where were the animals? Where was the rain? Still Noah obeyed God. They entered the ark and waited.

It wasn't long before they heard cawing, mooing, snorting, tweeting, and long, toothy jaws snapping. The animals came two by two. Giraffes, penguins, monkeys, rhinoceroses. Noah had never seen so many animals. When the last animal was safe inside the ark, God himself shut the doors.

Then the rain began. Slowly at first. Drip by drip. Then it began to pour. The seas rose. It rained for forty days and forty nights, until the whole earth was covered in water.

But the ark stayed afloat. Days passed into weeks and into months. At last the ark landed on a mountain peak poking out of the water. Three times Noah released a dove to look for land, and the third time, it did not return. It was time to get off the ark.

The first thing Noah and his family saw when they stepped on dry land was a rainbow stretched across the sky. It was a sign. A promise to Noah, his family, and everyone who came after—God would never again flood the earth with water.

Abraham

GENESIS 12-25; HEBREWS 11:8-19

 ". . . This is my covenant with you: You will be the father of many nations . . . your name will be Abraham . . ."
GENESIS 17:4-5 (NIV)

The city of Ur was big and wealthy. It had beautiful gardens, grand temples, and crowded markets where you could buy anything your heart desired. But when God commanded Abram, "Leave your country behind, and go to the land I show you," Abram packed up his family and left the city.

God promised to make Abram the father of many nations. His descendants would be as many as the stars in the sky and the sands on the seashore. All God asked was for Abram to trust and obey him. God even changed Abram's name to Abraham—"father of many."

Abraham didn't understand how it was going to happen. He was an old man, and his wife, Sarah, was old too. Still, they trusted God, and God kept His promise. After many years, Sarah had a son. They named him Isaac because he brought joy and laughter to their lives.

But that was not the end of Abraham's story. One day, God asked Abraham to sacrifice the one thing that was most precious to him—his only son Isaac. He wanted to see how much Abraham trusted him. And what do you think Abraham did? Even though he didn't understand and it caused him much pain, he set out to obey. He led Isaac up a mountain, built an altar, and prepared to offer his son to God. Before he harmed a hair on the boy's head, an angel grabbed his hand.

"Abraham! Abraham!" God called. "Do not hurt the boy. Now I know how much you trust me. Because you have obeyed my voice, you will be blessed, and through you all the nations of the earth will be blessed!"

For being ready to give up everything for God, Abraham became the father of many nations.

Sarah

GENESIS 12-25; HEBREWS 11:11-12

"Is anything too hard for the LORD? . . .
Sarah will have a son."

GENESIS 18:14 (NIV)

One day, three strangers arrived at the tents of Sarah and her husband, Abraham. It was a hot day. The strangers had been travelling for a long time and were tired and hungry. As soon as he saw them, Abraham rushed to Sarah's tent and told her to cook some barley cakes and fix drinks for their guests. He ordered one of his men to cook a bull. Soon Sarah had prepared a delicious meal.

While Abraham served the food, Sarah stayed in her tent. In those days, it was not polite for a woman to share food with foreign men. But she stood by the tent flap and listened to their conversation.

What they talked about confused Sarah. One of the strangers promised that Abraham and Sarah would soon have a son. When Sarah heard this, she laughed. How could this be? She was too old to have children. One of the men heard her. He looked at Abraham and asked, "Why does your wife laugh?"

Sarah realized these were not ordinary men. They were messengers from God. If they promised Sarah would have a son, then she would. The next spring, Sarah gave birth to a beautiful baby boy. Sarah and Abraham called him Isaac, which means "laughter," because he was the cause of their joy and laughter even in old age. Just as Abraham became the father of many nations, Sarah became their mother because she pleased God with her hospitable heart.

Jacob

 "Your name will no longer be Jacob but Israel, because you have struggled with God . . ."
GENESIS 32:28 (NIV)

Isaac and Rebekah had twin sons. They named the younger boy Jacob, "the Grabber," because he was always grabbing things. Even on the day he was born he was holding on to the ankle of his twin brother, Esau!

When they were grown up, Jacob grabbed something else from Esau. As the older son, Esau had a special birthright that he would inherit from their father. But one day when Esau was very hungry, Jacob convinced him to trade his birthright for a bowl of lentil stew. Later Jacob tricked his blind father by pretending to be Esau so he could get the firstborn blessing.

When Esau found out about Jacob's trick, he became angry. Jacob was afraid of what his brother might do to him so he ran away. He got married, had children, and became a very successful goatherd. Twenty years passed, then God told Jacob to go home.

But that meant he was going to have to face his brother. The night before their meeting, Jacob could not sleep so he went for a walk. Suddenly, he met someone who looked like a messenger of God. Jacob did what his name said—he ran up and grabbed him. They wrestled, and Jacob wouldn't let go. Even after his leg went limp, he still wouldn't let go.

"I won't let you go until you bless me," Jacob demanded.

The messenger asked, "What's your name?"

"Jacob."

"You won't be Jacob any longer," the messenger answered. "From now on, your name shall be Israel. For you have wrestled with God." Then he blessed Jacob and went away.

Now Jacob was no longer "the grabber." His name became the name of God's chosen people—Israel—and his sons' names became the names of Israel's twelve tribes.

Joseph

 You meant evil against me; but God meant it for good.
GENESIS 50:20 (NKJV)

Joseph had a great life. He had eleven brothers, ten older and one younger. His father loved him and gave him special gifts like a colorful new coat. And he had special talents like the ability to interpret dreams. But when he dreamed that his older brothers' wheat bowed down to him—meaning he would one day rule over them—they became so angry they threw him into a pit.

Joseph didn't think it could get worse, until a caravan of slave traders came along and bought him. They took Joseph to Egypt where he was sold as a slave to Potiphar.

Eventually, Joseph ended up in prison where he began to interpret dreams for his fellow prisoners. Soon Pharaoh heard about the wise young prisoner with special abilities. Pharaoh had been suffering from nightmares, so he summoned Joseph and told him his dreams. First, seven fat cows grazing by the river were eaten by seven scrawny cows! Then seven stalks of golden grain were swallowed up by seven withered stalks.

Immediately Joseph understood what the dreams were about. There were going to be seven years with lots of food. Then seven years of famine. Joseph told Pharaoh to spend the next seven years growing and storing as much food as Egypt could. Pharaoh agreed and put Joseph in charge.

When the famine came, it was so bad people travelled from all around to get food from Egypt. Even Joseph's own brothers arrived. They didn't recognize him because he looked like an Egyptian, but Joseph knew them right away. He could have punished them, but instead he gave them food and invited their families to Egypt so he could take care of them.

When at last Joseph revealed who he was, his brothers couldn't believe it. They were ashamed. Could Joseph ever forgive them? He did. "What you intended for evil," he told them, "God intended for good."

Moses

EXODUS 2-20; HEBREWS 11:23-29

 "I AM WHO I AM. This is what you say to the Israelites: I AM has sent you."

EXODUS 3:14 (NIV)

The last thing Moses wanted was to be a leader. Even though he had been raised in Pharaoh's palace, received the best education available, and enjoyed all the finest treasures of Egypt, he loved his simple shepherd's life in the desert.

One day while he was watching over his sheep, he stumbled upon a bush that was on fire, but it didn't burn up. The flames danced along the branches, but the leaves were as green as the day they sprouted. It was the strangest thing he had ever seen. When he stepped close, the bush spoke.

"Stop. Not another step. The ground you are standing on is holy ground. Take off your shoes." It was the voice of God. The Israelites, God's chosen people, were slaves in Egypt, and God wanted Moses to rescue them. "Go to Pharaoh," God said, "and say to him, 'Let my people go!'"

Moses didn't think the Israelites would follow him. But God promised to be with him always. "If anyone questions you, tell them, 'I AM' has sent you."

In the end, Moses obeyed. He went back to Pharaoh's palace and told him to let God's people go. When Pharaoh refused, God sent ten plagues—frogs, lice, locusts, hail, and more—until Pharaoh finally gave up. Then Moses led the Israelites out of Egypt.

Just as He promised, God was with Moses every step of the way. He parted the Sea of Reeds (also known as the Red Sea) so the people could walk on dry land. He provided food and water in the wilderness. He gave the Israelites Ten Commandments, the rules they would need to be a holy nation. And God gave Moses everything he needed to be a good leader.

Aaron

 . . . Their anointing shall surely be an everlasting priesthood throughout their generations.

EXODUS 40:15 (NKJV)

When God called Moses to free His people from Egypt, He promised to be with him. He also gave him a helper: his brother Aaron. When Moses first told Pharaoh to let God's people go, Aaron was right beside him. Every time Moses warned about a coming plague, Aaron went with him. When Moses led the Israelites through the Sea of Reeds, Aaron was at the front, right behind his brother. He was with Moses every step of the way.

But God had a special plan for Aaron too. If the Israelites were going to be God's special nation, they would have to be holy. And to stay holy, they would need someone to help them—to perform sacrifices, to burn the sacred incense, to care for the Tabernacle they were building. Someone who could speak to God on their behalf. They would need a high priest.

On the day Aaron was anointed high priest, he dressed in the finest blue robe, a colorful vest, and a breastplate made of all kinds of gems. On his forehead, he wore a golden band. Everything was made according to God's specifications. To be holy they had to do just as God commanded.

Then Moses poured oil over Aaron's head. It was a very special oil that smelled of cinnamon and sweet cassia and was made from a special recipe only for priests. It was the holiest oil in the land.

The same day Aaron was anointed, the Tabernacle was finished. Then God's glory came down and rested like a cloud in the Tabernacle. On that day, the Israelites knew they were God's holy people and that Aaron was his holy priest.

Miriam

EXODUS 2:1-8, 15:1-21

 Sing to the Lord, for He has triumphed gloriously!
The horse and rider He has thrown into the sea!

EXODUS 15:21 (NKJV)

Little Miriam helped her mother, Jochebed, make the most difficult choice she had ever made. Pharaoh's men were looking for all the baby boys of Israel. The only way Jochebed could save her son was to hide him in a reed basket in the Nile River. Miriam watched her mother lay the squirming baby into the basket. Jochebed kissed his forehead, covered the basket, and placed it in the water.

As the basket floated downstream, Miriam followed closely behind. When it nearly tipped over in the wake of Pharaoh's barge, Miriam was there to steady it. When it got stuck in a clump of papyrus reeds, she nudged it loose. At every stop and bend, with every twist and turn, she was by her brother's side.

Miriam was even there when the basket landed on the steps of Pharaoh's palace. She watched Pharaoh's daughter gently lift her brother out of the basket and kiss him on the forehead just like her mother had. Then Miriam knew he was going to be safe and sound.

Miriam continued to follow her brother even when they were grown up. His name was Moses, and he was the prophet who led God's people out of Egypt. Miriam was right behind him when he parted the Sea of Reeds. Moses held up his staff, the waters separated, and every last Israelite passed through on dry ground.

As soon as the Israelites reached the other side, Miriam picked up a tambourine and began to sing: "Sing to the Lord, for he has triumphed! His enemies are tossed into the sea." Soon all the other women joined in. They danced and shouted, their voices proclaiming God's strength and mercy. For all of this, Miriam was known as a prophetess of the Lord.

Joshua

DEUTERONOMY 31:1–8; JOSHUA 1–24; HEBREWS 11:30

 ". . . As for me and my household, we will serve the LORD."

JOSHUA 24:15 (NIV)

Although Moses led God's people up to the Promised Land, God chose Joshua to lead them in because he was faithful and brave. But entering the Promised Land was not going to be easy.

First, the Israelites had to cross the mighty Jordan River. When they saw the water crashing against the riverbanks, their eyes grew wide with fear. Not everyone could swim. There were small children and old people. And how would they get their supplies across?

God gave Joshua special instructions. The priests would enter the river first carrying the Ark of the Covenant, the sacred, golden chest that contained the Ten Commandments. It was a sign that God was always with them. When the soles of the priests' feet touched the water, the river stopped flowing! They carried the Ark into the middle of the riverbed and stood there while every man, woman, and child and all the animals passed by on dry ground.

Next came the city of Jericho with its mighty walls. The inhabitants were fierce warriors, descended from giants. Again, the Israelites were scared and again God gave instructions to Joshua. The army marched around the wall every day for seven days, and on the seventh day they marched around seven times. After the last march, the people shouted and the trumpets blew, and the walls of Jericho collapsed.

There were many more obstacles and enemies the Israelites had to face, but God was always with them. When at last the land was theirs, Joshua reminded the people of all God had done for them and about Abraham and Moses and the journey through the wilderness. When he was finished, he declared, "As for me and my house, we will serve the Lord." All the people agreed they would serve God as well.

Rahab

JOSHUA 2, 6:25; HEBREWS 11:31

*". . . Show kindness to my family, because
I have shown kindness to you."*

JOSHUA 2:12 (NIV)

Rahab knew who it was as soon as she heard the knock at the door. The king's guards. They were looking for two foreigners they saw snooping around her house. She told them she sent the strangers away. "They just left. If you go now, maybe you can catch them."

As soon as the door shut, Rahab raced to the roof. It was flat, open, and sunny, a good place to lay out anything to dry—wet laundry, grapes, and flax for making linen.

"They're gone," Rahab said in a loud whisper.

Suddenly, two men popped up from underneath the flax. Loose straw stuck to their hair. Rahab hung a rope down from her house, which sat on top of the wide city walls. The rope was just long enough to reach the ground. She motioned for the men to climb down.

"Why are you helping us?" they asked.

Rahab told them she knew who they were. All the people of Jericho did. They had heard the stories about the exodus from Egypt, crossing the Sea of Reeds, the battles against hostile kings. The city was afraid. But not Rahab. She believed that the God of the Israelites was also the God of heaven and earth. She made the men promise to spare her and her family when they returned to take the city.

One of them pointed to a bright red ribbon drying in the sun on the roof.

"Tie that ribbon in your window, and you will be spared. You and whoever is in your house."

Days later when the army of the Israelites returned to Jericho, they marched around the city walls for six days, and on the seventh they marched seven times around the city. At the end of the seventh march the priests blew their trumpets, the people shouted, and every last brick of the walls of Jericho tumbled to the ground. The Israelites took the city. But Rahab and her family were saved.

Deborah

JUDGES 4-5

*". . . May all who love you be like the sun
when it rises in its strength!"*
JUDGES 5:31 (NIV)

In the days before there were kings, prophets and judges ruled over the land of Israel. One of them was a wise woman named Deborah. Whenever a dispute arose between two people, they would go to her and plead their cases. Deborah would sit in the shade of a palm tree and listen carefully before giving her decision. The people never argued with her. They trusted her because she was always fair and just.

In those days, the Israelites were oppressed by a cruel general named Sisera. He had a large army with terrifying chariots. The Israelites had never seen men and horses move so quickly. Sisera's army could be heard coming from miles away. The earth trembled under the rumbling wheels. The Israelites prayed to God for a deliverer.

One day God told Deborah to summon a man named Barak and tell him to lead ten thousand Israelites against Sisera. Barak agreed but only if Deborah went with him.

If the Israelites were going to win, they would need a plan. Deborah and Barak led their army up a mountain. When Sisera's chariots got closer, they slowed down because of the steep slopes. At that moment, Deborah told Barak to attack. "This is the day the Lord gives Sisera into your hands! Hasn't the Lord gone ahead of you?"

Barak and all his men charged, and on that day they routed Sisera's army of chariots. Not a single one was left standing.

After the battle was done, Deborah and Barak sang a song of victory and praise to God: "May those who love the Lord shine like the sun when it rises in full strength!" Because Deborah and Barak trusted and obeyed God, there was peace in the land of Israel for the next forty years.

Gideon

 "A sword for the LORD and for Gideon!"

JUDGES 7:20 (NIV)

The Midianites had swarmed the land of Israel. They were taking people's land, eating up all the crops, stealing sheep and cows and whatever else they wanted. But God was going to free the Israelites.

One day an angel came to Gideon. "Gideon," the angel cried, "mighty warrior!" The angel told him that God had chosen him. But Gideon was afraid. He did not believe that God would choose a man from a poor family in a remote part of the country.

So Gideon tested God. That night he laid out a fleece and asked God to leave the ground dry but make the fleece wet with dew. In the morning the ground was completely dry, but the fleece was so wet that when he wrung it out Gideon filled a bowl with water.

But still Gideon didn't believe. So he tested God again. The next night he laid out the fleece, but this time he asked God to make the ground wet and leave the fleece dry. In the morning the ground was covered in dew, but there was not a drop of water on the fleece. Now Gideon was ready to do whatever God asked.

On a dark night, armed with nothing but a torch and a horn, Gideon led three hundred men to the Midianite camp. The men quietly crept around the camp and waited. As soon as Gideon lit his torch, they gave a loud battle cry, "A sword for the Lord and for Gideon!" The men blew their horns, and the whole camp was thrown into shock and confusion. In one night Gideon defeated the Midianites and freed God's people.

Samson

JUDGES 13-16; HEBREWS 11:32

 *The Spirit of the L*ORD *came powerfully upon him . . .*
JUDGES 14:6 (NIV)

For some time, Philistines ruled the land of Israel, and all the Israelites lived in fear except one. His name was Samson. He was the strongest man in the land. He was so strong he could kill a lion with his bare hands. He even fought a thousand Philistines with nothing but a donkey's jawbone. Everyone wanted to know how he got so strong. But it was a secret.

Now Samson was in love with a Philistine woman named Delilah, and she wanted to know his secret too. "Samson," she cooed, "is there anything stronger than you?" He told her to tie him down with strong, thick ropes. But it was a trick. He broke through the cords just by flexing his muscles.

Delilah was embarrassed. She asked him again, "Samson, tell me the truth. What's your weakness?" This time he told her to braid his hair in a loom. But it was another trick. Samson stood right up, and his hair snapped free.

Delilah had had enough. "If you really loved me, you would tell me your secret." This time Samson told her the truth. "My strength comes from God. I am sworn to Him from birth. No blade shall ever touch my hair. If my hair is cut, then my strength will leave me."

While Samson slept, Delilah cut his hair. When the Philistine soldiers came, they blinded him, chained him up, and took him prisoner. He did not have any strength to stop them.

But God did not forget Samson.

One day the Philistines chained Samson in the middle of a crowded temple with his hands on two pillars. They laughed and made fun of him. He asked God to give him strength one last time. He felt God's spirit swell inside him, and with all his might, he pushed on the pillars. The temple came crashing down right on top of everyone, including Samson. He gave his life just like he lived, full of strength and determination.

Ruth

 "Your people will be my people and your God my God."
RUTH 1:16 (NIV)

Ruth was a Moabite woman, but she married an Israelite. Her father-in-law and mother-in-law, Naomi, were all Israelites, but they lived in the land of Moab, because famine was ravaging their homeland. One day tragedy struck. Ruth's father-in-law died, then her husband. Now it was just Ruth and Naomi.

News came that the famine in Israel was over. Naomi was eager to go back home. She wanted to be with people who shared her language and way of life, people who worshipped her God. Ruth decided to go with her.

Naomi was surprised. She told Ruth to stay with her own people. But Ruth was insistent. "Where you go, I will go," she told Naomi. "Where you stay, I will stay. Your people will be my people, and your God will be my God. Where you die, I will die and be buried."

From that day forward, Ruth took care of Naomi. Even though they had practically nothing, she made sure Naomi had all she needed. She even had to beg for food and gather barley that was left for the poor at the edges of the fields.

One day Ruth was gathering barley in the field of a wealthy landowner named Boaz. As he watched how well she took care of Naomi, he fell in love with her. When he learned that Ruth was a widow, he asked her to marry him. Now Ruth and Naomi would be provided for the rest of their lives. Because Ruth chose to follow God and live with His people, He provided her with a new home, a new husband, and eventually a son.

Hannah

 "My heart rejoices in the LORD . . ."
1 SAMUEL 2:1 (NIV)

Hannah wanted a child more than anything else in the world. Day and night she prayed, begging God to give her a baby. Year after year she watched as other mothers cooed over newborn babies while she was left childless and sad.

One day Hannah and her husband went to the temple at Shiloh. After the service, Hannah stayed behind to pray. She promised God that if He would give her a baby, she would give the child back to Him. She prayed with great passion, but she was so brokenhearted no sound came out of her mouth.

A priest happened to notice her and thought she was drunk. "Woman, have you been drinking? This is the house of God. Put away your wine!" he scolded.

Hannah told him she was not drunk. She was just sad, and she was pouring out her sorrow to God. When he saw how she felt, the priest put his hand on her head and said, "Go in peace, and may God give you what you desire."

Not long after Hannah and her husband returned home, she discovered she was pregnant. Before the year was over she gave birth to a baby boy. She nursed him and raised him until he was old enough to leave home.

Then Hannah did just like she promised. She took her son back to the temple and left him in the care of the kind, old priest. But she was not sad as she left. She began to sing, "My heart rejoices, and my voice sings long. There is none holy as you. No rock so sturdy or strong. Oh my God, you are my salvation."

Hannah's son was named Samuel. He learned to serve the Lord and grew up to be one of the mightiest prophets of God.

Samuel

1 SAMUEL 3; HEBREWS 11:32

 "Speak, Lord, for your servant is listening."
1 SAMUEL 3:9 (NIV)

The first time Samuel heard God's voice he had no idea who it was. He had been living at the temple for a few years and had learned how to take care of the place. He kept it clean and holy. He was a hard worker and an obedient child.

Late one night, he heard someone calling his name. "Samuel. Samuel."

He ran to the old priest, Eli, and woke him up. "Here I am. You were calling me."

"No, I wasn't," Eli snapped. He didn't like being woken up in the middle of the night. He ordered Samuel back to bed.

Once more the voice called, "Samuel. Samuel."

The boy rushed to Eli again. The old man was starting to get very annoyed.

But when it happened a third time, Eli told Samuel to go back to bed and when he heard the voice again say, "Speak, Lord. Your servant is listening."

Samuel did as he was told. When he heard the voice call, "Samuel. Samuel" he said, "Speak, Lord. Your servant is listening."

Then the Lord spoke to Samuel.

That night was the first time God talked with him, but it would not be the last. When Samuel was grown up, he became one of God's mightiest prophets. He preached wherever he went, and his words never failed. He anointed the first king of Israel, King Saul, and the second, the mighty King David. He lived a long life, always listening to the voice of God.

David

1 SAMUEL 16-18; 2 SAMUEL 2, 7-8; HEBREWS 11:32

 "I have found David, son of Jesse, a man after my own heart."

ACTS 13:22 (NIV)

Every day the Philistine giant Goliath taunted the Israelites in the battlefield, "I defy the armies of Israel and their God!" The man was so big no one wanted to face him. Not the king or any of his men. But a shepherd boy named David couldn't believe someone would dare talk about God's people like that! The giant had to be silenced. David volunteered.

The king tried to give David his armor, but it was too big. He tried to give him a sword and shield, but they were too heavy. All he had was a staff and sling and five smooth river stones. Besides, David had a secret weapon—the spirit of God. Months earlier the prophet Samuel had come to his house and anointed him with oil. As soon as the oil touched David's forehead, God's power came over him. From that day forward, he was filled with wisdom and courage and all the gifts of the Lord.

The next day Goliath went back to the battlefield. The earth quaked with each footstep. All the king's men trembled with fear. But David stood firm, his eyes fierce.

Goliath took one look at the boy and laughed. "Am I a dog that you come at me with sticks and stones?"

David answered, "I come at you in the name of the Lord." Then he put a stone in his sling and spun it overhead, around and around, as the giant stamped closer. As soon as Goliath was in range, David let it go. The stone hit Goliath right in the forehead. Instantly, the giant fell dead. The Israelites were saved!

Years later David became Israel's mightiest king, defeating all her enemies just like Goliath. He made the land safe and secure. He wrote beautiful psalms declaring his love for the Lord. He loved God so much he was called "a man after God's own heart."

Solomon

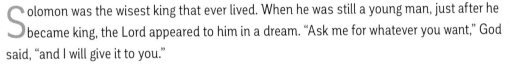

"So give your servant a discerning heart to govern your people and to distinguish right from wrong."

1 KINGS 3:9 (NIV)

Solomon was the wisest king that ever lived. When he was still a young man, just after he became king, the Lord appeared to him in a dream. "Ask me for whatever you want," God said, "and I will give it to you."

Solomon could have asked for anything: a mighty army, all the money in the world, a kind and beautiful woman to be his wife, but instead he asked for wisdom. "I am still a child," Solomon said, "and don't know how to be king. Give me prudence so that I can tell right from wrong and govern your people well."

The king's answer pleased God so much that He promised not just to give him wisdom but all the things Solomon had not asked for. "I will give you wealth and honor," God promised, "and make you mightier than any other king."

Solomon loved God so much he wanted to build Him a beautiful temple. He hired the best carpenters and stonecutters. He bought the finest cedar wood and the smoothest stone. And everything was overlaid with gold. It was the most beautiful building the people had ever seen. A perfect house for the Ark of the Covenant, the sacred chest that held God's law.

News of Solomon's wisdom and the beautiful temple spread throughout the world. People came from all around to bring gifts and honor the king. Because Solomon loved God above everything else and desired wisdom, God blessed him more than he ever could have imagined.

Elijah and Elisha

1 KINGS 17–19; 2 KINGS 1–2

 "Lord, the God of Abraham, Isaac and Israel, let it be known today that you are God in Israel and that I am your servant."

1 KINGS 18:36 (NIV)

Elijah was one of the greatest prophets in the history of Israel. He was filled with God's spirit, performing many miracles and preaching that the God of Israel was the one, true God.

Once there was a contest where four hundred fifty priests prayed as loudly as they could to their god. Nothing happened. Then Elijah prayed and as soon as he finished speaking, fire fell from heaven and ignited the altar. Only his God deserved worship.

But Queen Jezebel worshipped the same god as the helpless priests. She wanted Elijah arrested and put to death. So Elijah fled to the wilderness. After walking all day, he laid down under a tree asking God if he could just die. But God provided bread and water and asked him why he was hiding in the wilderness.

"I'm all alone," Elijah answered. "The king and queen are trying to kill me."

God told him to go to the mountain and wait for Him to pass by. First a powerful whirlwind came, but God was not in the wind. Then the earth shook, but God was not in the earthquake. Then a raging wildfire passed by, but God was not in the fire. Finally, Elijah heard a soft, quiet whisper. As soon as he heard it, he knew God was in the whisper.

The next day Elijah left the wilderness and went back to Israel, where he met a young man named Elisha. Elijah would not be alone anymore. Elisha followed Elijah until the day Elijah was taken into heaven by a chariot of fire. As Elisha watched Elijah ascend until he couldn't see him anymore, he noticed a brown cloth floating down to the ground. It was Elijah's cloak. As soon as he put it on, Elisha was filled with God's spirit. From that day on, he carried on Elijah's mission of performing miracles and preaching that the God of Israel was the one, true God.

Jonah

JONAH 1-4

 ". . . you are a gracious and compassionate God, slow to anger and abounding in love . . ."

JONAH 4:2 (NIV)

The last thing Jonah wanted to do was preach to the people of Nineveh. He had heard stories about how they ransacked cities, kidnapped women and children, and took whatever they wanted. If anyone deserved to be punished by God, it was the Ninevites. But God told Jonah to go to Nineveh and tell them to repent. Instead, Jonah got in a ship heading as far away from Nineveh as possible.

Suddenly the ship was hit by a storm. Huge waves crashed onto the deck. Wind ripped through the sails. The captain told everyone to pray to see who was punishing them. Jonah knew whose fault it was. "I serve the God of land and sea," he said. "If you want to be saved, you must throw me overboard." The sailors didn't want to, but they followed his instructions. As soon as Jonah's toes hit the water, the storm stopped.

Just when Jonah thought things couldn't get any worse, he noticed a large shadow swimming in the murky waters below. Out of the blue, the creature raced to the surface and swallowed him whole! Now Jonah was trapped in the belly of a big fish. Smelly and wet, he couldn't see a thing. The only thing he could do was pray to God to save him. For three days and three nights, the fish swam until it reached shore and spat Jonah out, right back where he started.

Now Jonah went to Nineveh and told the people to repent from their wicked ways. And do you know what they did? They repented. The king himself declared a day of fasting and prayer. God forgave them of their sins. That day Jonah learned it doesn't matter how far you run from God, He's ready to forgive when you turn back to Him.

Huldah

2 KINGS 13:22-30; 2 CHRONICLES 34:22-28

 *"You made yourself humble in the eyes of the Lord.
. . . And I have heard you,"* announces the Lord.

2 KINGS 22:19 (NIRV)

Huldah was a mighty prophetess, who spoke God's will to the king. God's temple was falling apart after years of neglect. The stone walls were crumbling, wood rotting, the gold and silver tarnished. But worst of all, the Torah, the scrolls containing God's Law, was lost. No one knew where to find them.

King Josiah wanted to rebuild the temple. He didn't care how much it would cost. He wanted it to be as beautiful as ever. While the builders were working in the temple, someone stumbled upon the most beautiful surprise of all—the Torah. God's Law. It was buried deep in the temple treasury.

King Josiah was overjoyed until he read some of it. For years, the people of Judah had disobeyed God's Law and worshipped false gods. He wondered if God would punish them, even after all that he had done to please Him. The king sent his priest to ask Huldah if she knew God's plan.

Huldah was brave and filled with the spirit. "This is what the Lord, God of Israel says." Her voice was strong and her eyes fierce. "'My anger burns and will not be quenched. God will bring judgment and punishment upon the land of Judah."

Then her voice grew quiet and her face softened. "But the king should not be afraid. Tell him that he has done what's pleasing in the eyes of God and he will be spared. None of this shall come to pass until he had joined his fathers in eternal rest." As God's prophetess, Huldah knew how eagerly the Lord wanted to show mercy to whomever was humble and listened to His word.

Shadrach, Meshach, and Abednego

DANIEL 3; HEBREWS 11:34

Our God whom we serve is able to deliver us from the burning fiery furnace.

DANIEL 3:17 (NKJV)

King Nebuchadnezzar wanted everyone to know how important he was. He had a huge statue of himself built. It was over ninety feet tall and made of pure gold! The king ordered the people to bow down and worship the statue as soon as they heard special music play.

When the trumpets blared and the drums beat, everyone fell face down on the ground except three young men: Shadrach, Meshach, and Abednego. Because they were Jews, God's chosen people, they refused to worship anyone or anything except God Himself.

When King Nebuchadnezzar heard this, he became angry. He had the men arrested and threatened to throw them into a fiery furnace. But they refused to change their minds.

"If you throw us into the furnace, our God will save us," they said. "But even if He doesn't, we will not serve your gods or worship your statue of gold."

When Nebuchadnezzar heard these words, he flew into a rage and ordered the furnace heated seven times hotter. Shadrach, Meshach, and Abednego were tied up with ropes so tight they cut into their skin and then thrown into the fire.

When the guards went to check on them, they saw something strange. Instead of three men in the furnace, they saw four. The fourth looked like an angel or son of God.

When the king looked in, he immediately knew he had made a mistake. He ordered Shadrach, Meshach, and Abednego to come out. When they stepped out, not a hair on their bodies was singed. That day, King Nebuchadnezzar praised their God. All of this because three young men trusted God and obeyed Him above all else.

Daniel

DANIEL 1–6; HEBREWS 11:33

 He is the living God and steadfast forever; His kingdom is the one which shall not be destroyed.

DANIEL 6:27 (NKJV)

Daniel was King Darius's most trusted advisor. He had advised kings before Darius, interpreting dreams and prophesying things to come. Everything Daniel said was full of wisdom and understanding. The king loved Daniel so much the other advisors were jealous and plotted to have him killed. But they could find nothing to accuse him of because he did nothing wrong. So they convinced King Darius to pass a law that no one was allowed to pray or worship anyone except the king for thirty days. Whoever disobeyed would be thrown into a den of hungry lions.

Many were afraid of the law and prayed only to the king, but not Daniel. He prayed just as he always had: three times a day standing at his window, facing Jerusalem, his home.

It was not long before Daniel was arrested and taken before the king. When King Darius realized he had been tricked, he was upset. But the law was the law and could not be undone, not even by the king. Daniel had to be thrown into the lions' den. "May the God you serve save you!" King Darius said to his friend.

A huge stone was rolled in front of the den and sealed with the king's ring. That night, King Darius could not sleep, he was so worried about Daniel. At dawn, he hurried to the lions' den. "Daniel! Daniel!" the king called.

He waited. Was he dead? Then through the thick stone he heard Daniel's voice. "My God sent an angel to the shut the lions' mouths, and there isn't a scratch on me."

King Darius was thrilled. He ordered Daniel to be removed from the den. And he made a new law that everyone in the kingdom should respect and worship Daniel's God, because He was the true and living God.

Ezra

EZRA 1–10

 "The gracious hand of our God is on everyone who looks to him ..."

EZRA 8:22 (NIV)

Ezra was a very respected Israelite in Persia. He lived in the blue-stoned city of Babylon, a city famous for knowledge and science. His family descended from Aaron, the first high priest, and like his ancestors Ezra knew the Law of Moses. But he was not happy. He wanted to go home. He wanted to go back to Jerusalem to worship at the newly built temple of God.

After receiving permission from the king, Ezra invited other Israelites who could serve the Lord at the temple: priests, Levites, musicians, even gatekeepers. They gathered at the banks of the Euphrates River. The journey was going to be hard and dangerous. They were carrying lots of gold and silver and other supplies for the temple. Some worried about bandits stealing the sacred treasure. Maybe they should ask the king for soldiers to protect them.

But Ezra refused. He reminded the Israelites that God was all the protection they needed. "His hand is on everyone who seeks Him, and his anger against those who forsake Him." Ezra declared a fast and told everyone to ask God for a safe journey. Then he selected twelve priests and consecrated them. He entrusted them with the temple treasures, "Guard these until you reach the house of the Lord."

After twelve days of fasting and praying, Ezra and the Israelites finally set out. It took them five long months to reach Jerusalem, but God was with them the whole way. He protected them from every threat and danger. When at last they reached the city, Ezra and the priests took the sacred gold and silver to the temple. There everyone gathered to offer a sacrifice and thank God for guiding them with His gracious hand.

Esther

*"Yet who knows whether you have come to
the kingdom for such a time as this?"*
ESTHER 4:14 (NKJV)

King Xerxes was so angry with his wife he wanted a new one. He held a contest to find the most beautiful woman in Persia. After months of searching, a new queen was chosen. Her name was Esther, but she had a secret no one knew—not even the king. Esther was a Jew.

Xerxes's advisor, Haman, did not like the Jews. He tricked the king into signing a law that every Jewish man, woman, and child in all of Persia would be put to death. Queen Esther didn't know what to do. If she said nothing, her friends and family and all her people would be put to death. But if she told the king her secret, it could make him so angry he would put her to death.

Esther asked her uncle Mordecai what to do. He told her to be brave. "Who knows? Perhaps you were crowned queen for such a time as this."

Queen Esther decided to host a dinner in honor of the king. The food was delicious, the wine plentiful, and she looked more beautiful than ever. King Xerxes was so pleased he asked if there was anything she wanted.

"O my king," she said, "if I've pleased you, then spare my life and the lives of my people."

When he heard this, he was shocked. Who was threatening her? Who were her people?

Bravely, Esther looked the king in the eye and told him she was a Jew.

When King Xerxes realized he had signed an evil law, he punished Haman, the man who tricked him, but he could not get rid of the signed law. Instead, he passed a new one that gave Jews permission to defend themselves. He even told the governors to help them. When the dreaded day came, not a single Jew was harmed. By her honesty and bravery, Queen Esther had saved her people.

Jesus

 "And the Word became flesh and dwelt among us."

JOHN 1:14 (ESV)

In the beginning only God existed. God the Father, Son, and Holy Spirit. One day God—God the Son—became a man. That man's name is Jesus.

This is what we believe about Jesus.

Before he became man, Jesus was already God's son. He existed before all time. He was not created like you and me, but He is the Creator just as much as God the Father. Everything was made by Him.

In the years of the Roman Empire, Jesus became a human. He was born to a Jewish woman named Mary. Even though she was not married, she became pregnant by the power of the Holy Spirit. Her baby, Jesus, was born so that He could save all people. He showed us how to love God and love each other. He preached to crowds of people and performed many miracles: making the blind see, the lame walk, even raising the dead. He cared for the poor.

One day Jesus was arrested and condemned to die by the Roman governor. He was led outside the city and nailed to a cross. That was how many criminals were executed back then. But Jesus was not a criminal; He had done nothing wrong. Jesus died because we had done wrong. He died for our sins. But Jesus did not stay dead. Three days later He rose. He spent forty days with His disciples preaching and performing more miracles, until He went back to heaven where He sits next to His Father.

Jesus is the Christ, the Messiah, the Anointed One, chosen by God. He is our Lord and Savior, and one day He will come again to judge everyone who has ever lived. He will rule over a glorious and perfect kingdom—a kingdom that will never end!

Mary

MATTHEW 1-2; LUKE 1-2; JOHN 2

 "Let it be to me according to your word."

LUKE 1:38 (ESV)

It all started with a yes.

Mary was a young woman preparing to get married when an angel appeared out of nowhere. He told her she was very special. Of all the women in the world, God had picked her to have His son. Mary was going to have a baby! She was confused. How could she have a baby when she wasn't married? Even so, Mary said yes. For this, she was called "the most blessed among women." She gave birth in a stable, where she was visited by shepherds and a chorus of angels. Eight days later, she and her husband presented the baby at God's temple. They named him Jesus.

Mary worried about her son and kept a close eye on Him. When He was only twelve, He stayed at the temple to talk to the priests and teachers without her realizing it. When He was an adult, Jesus went into the desert alone for forty days and forty nights, but Mary couldn't go with Him to take care of Him. All she could do was pray. When He returned, she even convinced Jesus to do His first miracle. She was an attentive and loving mother.

One night Mary heard her son had been arrested and taken before the governor where He was whipped and crowned with sharp thorns. As Jesus carried a heavy cross out of the city, she walked with Him every step of the way. She stood under the cross as He breathed his last breath.

But Mary never lost faith. She reminded Jesus's friends that He promised to come again. She rejoiced when He appeared three days later. She was there when the Holy Spirit came down at Pentecost. As the woman God chose to be Jesus's mother, Mary was always looking forward to the day she would be gloriously reunited with her son.

Joseph

Joseph was a just man . . .

MATTHEW 1:19 (NCB)

In the town of Nazareth lived a humble carpenter named Joseph. He could make all kinds of things with his hands: tables, chairs, and even children's toys. Joseph was a good and just man. He was fair to all his customers. He treated everyone with dignity and respect. He also loved God with all his heart, soul, and mind.

Joseph was engaged to a young woman named Mary. But Mary had a secret. She was going to have a baby. When he learned about the child, Joseph did not know what to do. He knew the Torah, the Law of Moses. If a woman was found pregnant before marriage, she could be punished, disgraced, even put to death. He did not want that to happen. But he was not sure he wanted to marry her either. Night after night he lay awake tossing and turning, wrestling with his thoughts. What should he do?

One night an angel came to Joseph in a dream. The angel said to Joseph, "Don't be afraid. Take Mary as your wife. The child she has conceived is from God, the Holy Spirit."

When he awoke, Joseph did what the angel said. He took Mary as his wife and raised the boy as his own son. Joseph taught him to be good and just and pious, to treat others the way he would want to be treated, and to love God with all his heart, soul, and mind. The boy grew up wise, strong, and brave. His name was Jesus.

Zechariah and Elizabeth

LUKE 1:5-56

 Both of them were righteous in the sight of God, observing all the Lord's commands . . .

LUKE 1:6 (NIV)

Zechariah and Elizabeth were a righteous couple. They loved God and obeyed His laws. Zechariah was the temple priest. They lived in a nice home and were very happy except for one thing. They had no children. For years, they prayed for a child. Now they were too old.

One day Zechariah was burning incense at the altar when an angel appeared and said, "Don't be afraid. Your prayers have been answered." Elizabeth was going to have a son, and the angel said to name him John. But Zechariah didn't believe it. How could Elizabeth have a child when she was so old? The angel scolded him, "Because you did not believe, you will be unable to speak until your son is born."

Elizabeth became pregnant, just as the angel promised. Now, her cousin, Mary, who was pregnant with baby Jesus, was coming to visit. While Mary was still outside, she called to Elizabeth. The moment Elizabeth heard her voice, she felt the baby leap in her belly. Even he was excited that Mary and Jesus were coming! Elizabeth dropped what she was doing and ran outside. She called to Mary, "Blessed are you among women! And blessed is the fruit of your womb!"

Soon it was time for Elizabeth to give birth. Everyone was excited. Family came; the neighbors gathered. They all thought the baby would be named after his father. But Elizabeth said no. When they asked Zechariah, he signaled for a tablet and wrote, "His name is John." At that moment, Zechariah could speak again. The first thing he did was sing to God: "Praise the Lord, God of Israel, because he has come to his people and set them free!" Zechariah and Elizabeth were filled with joy—God had blessed them with a baby boy.

John the Baptist

 "I am the voice of one calling in the wilderness . . ."
JOHN 1:23 (NIV)

It must have been difficult to be Jesus's cousin. As Jesus did more and more miracles, and more and more people followed him, it would have been easy to get jealous. But John the Baptist knew his job was important too—lead others to Jesus.

Before John was born, an angel visited his father, Zechariah, and told him John was chosen to be a prophet of God. While still in his mother's womb, John felt the stir of the Holy Spirit when Mary visited Elizabeth. When he grew up, he went to live in the desert. He wanted to get away from the distractions and temptations of the city. All he ate were locusts and wild honey. People came to the desert to hear him preach and be baptized. "Repent," he said. "The kingdom of heaven is coming!" When someone asked if he was the long-awaited messiah, he said, "No. I am just a voice. The voice of someone shouting in the wilderness."

One day a man came down to the river to be baptized. John recognized Him as soon as he saw Him. It was Jesus, his cousin. "Look!" John shouted to the crowds. "The Lamb of God, who takes away the sins of the world."

John didn't think he should baptize Jesus. "You should baptize me," he said. But Jesus was insistent. As Jesus's head came out of the water, the skies opened up, a dove came down from heaven, and a voice spoke, "This is my beloved Son in whom I am well pleased." From that day forward, John continued to preach his message of repentance and forgiveness and spread the news about his cousin Jesus.

John

MATTHEW 4:18-22; LUKE 5:1-11; JOHN 19:25-27

 Dear friends, let us love one another . . . because God is love.

1 JOHN 4:7, 8 (NIV)

Even Jesus had best friends. One of His very best friends was John. He was called "the disciple whom Jesus loved."

John grew up in a fishing town on the shores of the Sea of Galilee. His father, Zebedee, was a successful fisherman. They were a respected family, even friends with the high priest in Jerusalem. John and his brother, James, worked for their father. They spent long hours under the stars casting their nets into the cool, quiet waters of Galilee. In the morning, they cleaned the nets and took the fish to market.

One morning, while John and James were gathering up the nets on the seashore, Rabbi Jesus was passing by. He called out to them, "Come. Follow me." Immediately they dropped what they were doing and followed Him. They became two of Jesus's disciples.

John followed Jesus everywhere, even when many of the other disciples weren't around. When Jesus revealed His glory on the Mount of Transfiguration, only John, Peter, and James witnessed it. When Jesus raised a girl from the dead, only they were with Him again. And when Jesus said His last prayers in the garden of Gethsemane, He asked these three friends to stay by his side.

At the end, John was the person Jesus trusted to look after His mother. As He hung on the cross breathing His last, Jesus told him, "John, here is your mother." Then He told Mary to take care of John. "Mother, see your son." John took her home and from that day forward cared for her like his own mother.

Mary and Martha

LUKE 10:38-42; JOHN 12:1-10

 Mary has chosen the better part, and it will not be taken away from her.

LUKE 10:42 (NABRE)

Jesus had no home. He once said, "Foxes have holes, and birds have nests, but I have no place to lay my head." So whenever he visited Jerusalem, he needed a place to stay, and his favorite place to visit was the house of Lazarus.

Lazarus had two sisters—Martha and Mary. They lived together in a small house just outside Jerusalem in a humble neighborhood called Bethany. Whenever Jesus came to visit, Martha and Mary liked to offer Him a sumptuous feast.

One day, after Jesus arrived, Martha busily prepared the meal while Mary sat and talked to him. She left Martha to do all the work herself.

After making the bread and setting the table, Martha was starting to get annoyed. Where was her sister? Why wasn't she helping? Finally she couldn't take it anymore. She stormed into the room where Jesus and Mary were sitting. "Lord, doesn't it bother you that my sister is making me do all the work?" she said. "Why don't you tell her to help?"

Jesus smiled and answered, "Martha, you worry about too many things. There is only one thing that really matters, and Mary has chosen what's best. You can't take that from her."

Jesus did not ask his followers to *do* anything for him. He only longed to be with them. Just like Mary. Sitting at his feet. Listening to His words. Sharing their hearts with Him.

Lazarus

JOHN 11:1-46

 Jesus said to her, "I am the resurrection and the life . . ."

JOHN 11:25 (NIV)

One day Jesus received news that His dear friend Lazarus was very sick. His sisters, Mary and Martha, were afraid he was going to die. They asked Jesus to come to Bethany as quickly as possible. But Jesus wasn't worried. He knew God had other plans for Lazarus. So Jesus stayed where He was for a couple more days.

By the time Jesus and His disciples reached Bethany, Lazarus was dead. He had been buried for four days. Martha and Mary were very sad. Many of their friends had come to comfort them. When the sisters saw Jesus, they ran up to him. "If only you had been here, our brother would not have died," they cried. Seeing the sorrow of all the people mourning, Jesus became so upset he started to cry. He asked where Lazarus was laid, and they showed Him the tomb.

"Roll away the stone," Jesus commanded.

"But it's been four days," Martha protested. "The body is already decaying."

But Jesus insisted. As soon as the tomb was opened, He said a prayer to God. Then He shouted in a loud voice, "Lazarus, come out!"

At first nothing happened. The tomb was dark and quiet. Everyone waited. What would happen? Jesus couldn't really call a man back from the dead—could he? Suddenly, a figure appeared at the entrance. You couldn't see his face because he was wrapped in graveclothes from head to toe.

"Unwrap him! Let him go!" Jesus called.

They pulled the cloth down from his face, and there he was—Lazarus! Alive again! On that day Martha, Mary, and all the disciples saw that Jesus was the resurrection and the life. He had power even over death.

Zacchaeus

LUKE 19:1–10

 Jesus said to him, "Today salvation has come to this house!"
LUKE 19:9 (NIV)

Zacchaeus had one of the most despised jobs in Judea: a tax collector. He collected money from his fellow Jews to give to the Roman rulers. It made him rich but he was one of the most hated men in town.

One day Zacchaeus heard that Rabbi Jesus was coming to town. He knew all the stories about him: the amazing miracles, the beautiful sermons, and how he cared for the poor. He didn't think Jesus would want anything to do with him, but perhaps he could catch a glimpse.

The streets were crowded. Zacchaeus was too short to see anything. Then he got an idea. A tall sycamore tree with long, low branches stood near the main road. Zacchaeus shimmied up the tree and found a nice spot to watch the road. The large sycamore leaves would hide him from view. He didn't want anyone to see him in the embarrassing position.

Zacchaeus could already see Jesus coming down the road with people following close behind. When Jesus reached the spot right below Zacchaeus, He did the last thing Zacchaeus wanted. He looked up.

The crowd noticed the tax collector too. They laughed and made fun of him and called him names. But Jesus did not. He looked at him with warm, friendly eyes like no one else ever had.

At last Jesus spoke, "Zacchaeus, come down! I'm going to your house today!"

Zacchaeus couldn't believe his ears. Jesus, the miracle-worker, the beloved rabbi, one of the most famous men in Judea, wanted to come to his house! He climbed down and welcomed Jesus into his home. He promised to be a better man, to care for the poor, and treat everyone fairly. Jesus declared, "Today, salvation has come to this house!"

The Roman Centurion

MATTHEW 27:33-55; MARK 15:22-41;

LUKE 23:33-49; JOHN 19:16-30

*[The centurion] said, ". . . Surely, this
man was the Son of God!"*

MARK 15:39 (NIV)

The centurion had overseen many crucifixions. Like any commander in the Roman army, he had to be tough. His job was to keep order. Sometimes this meant arresting people and even putting them to death. One day he oversaw a crucifixion he never forgot.

Three criminals were supposed to be crucified. But one had many followers. The other guards were afraid these followers might cause trouble. But the man told His followers to put their swords away. "Whoever lives by the sword dies by the sword."

Even though the centurion had witnessed hundreds of crucifixions, he never saw one like this. The man held His head high as He carried his cross. His back was scarred with whiplashes, and His forehead bled where it was pierced by a crown of thorns. Soldiers kept jabbing and taunting Him. At one point, the man fell down and couldn't get back up so someone else had to carry the cross the rest of the way.

When they reached the hill where the criminals were supposed to be crucified, the centurion ordered their hands and feet nailed to the crosses. The other two men screamed in pain. But this man did not make a noise. He was as quiet as a lamb.

At last the cross was raised. The man's followers were watching and crying, even His own mother. Others came to mock Him. From the cross, the man spoke only of forgiveness. With His final breath, He prayed, "Father, into your hands I commend my spirit." At that moment, the ground shook, and the sky became dark even though it was the middle of the day. When he saw what happened, the centurion realized this was no ordinary man.

"Surely this man was the Son of God!" he said.

Mary Magdalene

LUKE 8:2; LUKE 24:1-10; JOHN 19:25-20:18

 Mary Magdalene went to the disciples with the news: "I have seen the Lord!"

JOHN 20:18 (NIV)

From the day Jesus began His ministry, several women followed Him. One was Mary Magdalene. Before she met Jesus, Mary was a troubled woman. Some even said she was possessed by demons. Then Jesus healed her: body and soul. From that day, she followed Him and became one of His closest friends.

Mary Magdalene was near when Jesus was sentenced to die. She watched Him carry the cross to Calvary. She saw the soldiers hammer nails through His hands and feet. She was at the foot of the cross when He said His last words: "It is finished." She even helped prepare Jesus's body for burial.

Three days after Jesus's death, Mary Magdalene went back to the tomb with spices and scented oils to anoint His body. But when she got there, the tomb was empty. The body was gone! What had they done with Him? She ran to tell Jesus's other followers right away.

Mary went back to search for Jesus. Suddenly she saw a stranger in the garden. Since it was early morning, she thought He was a groundskeeper. The stranger asked why she was crying. She told Him she was looking for the body of Jesus.

"If you know where they've put Him, tell me so I can take Him away," she begged.

Then the stranger said her name, "Mary."

At that moment, Mary Magdalene realized she was talking to Jesus. "Rabbi!" she called. Her tears of sorrow turned into tears of joy. He instructed her to tell the other disciples the good news. And that's just what she did. Mary Magdalene was the first person to tell others that Jesus was risen!

Thomas

JOHN 20:19-29

 Thomas said to him, "My Lord and my God!"
JOHN 20:28 (NIV)

Even though he had been with Jesus for three years, Thomas still had doubts. He was there when Jesus turned water into wine. He was there when He raised their friend Lazarus from the dead. He had seen Him make the lame walk and the blind see. He watched Him tell a storm to quiet down. He had listened to Jesus preach beautiful words like, "Blessed are the peacemakers, for they shall see God" and "Love one another as I have loved you." Thomas was with Jesus when He said, "Take. Eat. This is my body. This is my blood."

But when the women said that Jesus had risen from the dead, that they had seen Him, it was too much. Thomas couldn't believe what he was hearing. All the disciples were ecstatic. "He is risen! He is risen!" But Thomas shook his head. It was impossible. A man could not just rise from the dead.

"Unless I put my hand in His side and my fingers where the nails pierced Him, I can't believe," Thomas said.

Suddenly everyone in the room gasped and became still. No one said a word. A voice behind Thomas spoke, "Then turn around and place your hand here."

Thomas turned around. It was Jesus! Where had He come from? How did He get here? It didn't matter. Thomas ran to Him and threw his arms around him. He hugged him tightly. Jesus was alive just liked He promised.

"My Lord and my God," was all he could say.

Jesus held Thomas by the shoulders and looked him in the eyes. "You believe, because you have seen," He said, "but blessed are those who do not see and still believe."

Peter

MATTHEW 14:22–36, 16:13–20, 26:69–75

 [Jesus said], ". . . you are Peter, and upon this rock I will build my church . . ."
MATTHEW 16:18 (NIV)

Upon this rock I will build my church!"

With these words, Jesus gave His disciple, Simon, a new name. Now he would be called Peter. The Rock. And Jesus wanted him to lead His church.

Peter had great faith, but he was often afraid. Once Jesus invited Peter to walk with him on the water. Peter followed until he got distracted by the wind and waves and began to sink. Thankfully, Jesus caught him before he drowned.

On the night Jesus was arrested and put on trial, Peter waited outside. He was worried about his teacher. When a woman asked him if he was one of Jesus's followers, Peter shook his head. He was too scared to say yes. She kept questioning him. In fear, Peter denied Jesus not once or twice but three times. As dawn broke and the rooster crowed, he realized what he had done.

All that changed when the Holy Spirit came down at Pentecost. Jesus's followers were filled with the Spirit, including Peter. Tongues of fire danced on their foreheads. They began to speak in all kinds of languages. When they went outside, people started making fun of them. Some even said they were drunk.

That day Peter found his voice. He wasn't scared anymore. "No. These men are not drunk," he said. "They are filled with the Spirit of God just like the prophets of old." Then he preached about Jesus: how He died, was buried, and rose again, and that He was the Messiah, the Son of the living God. That day three thousand people believed and were baptized, and Jesus's church was born!

Stephen

ACTS 6–7

 But Stephen, full of the Holy Spirit, looked up to heaven and saw the glory of God . . .

ACTS 7:55 (NIV)

Stephen was one of the first deacons of the fast-growing, new church. After Jesus ascended to heaven and the Holy Spirit came down, the apostles began to preach all over the Roman Empire. So many new people wanted to be baptized that the apostles couldn't take care of them all. So they appointed seven men as deacons. Their job was to make sure everyone had what they needed: food to eat, clothes to wear, and a place to live.

Because he was filled with faith and the Holy Spirit, Stephen began to anger those who did not believe in Jesus. Finally, they arrested him and took him to the judges in Jerusalem called the Sanhedrin. He was accused of saying bad things about Moses and God, but it wasn't true. The Sanhedrin argued with him, yelling angrily. They scowled, but Stephen's face shone like an angel. He knew God was with him.

When it was Stephen's turn to speak, he said the Sanhedrin were the ones who displeased God because they hadn't listened to Jesus and had put Him to death. The Sanhedrin became so angry they dragged him out of the city and hurled large stones at him. Stephen fell to the ground bruised and bloodied, but he asked God to forgive the very men who were throwing the stones. His words were calm and peaceful. He prayed, "Lord Jesus, receive my spirit," then closed his eyes. Stephen was the first person to die for his faith in Jesus. Not only was he one of the first deacons, he was also the first martyr.

Paul

ACTS 9:1-31

*Grace and peace to you from God our Father
and from the Lord Jesus Christ.*
ROMANS 1:7 (NIV)

Paul wasn't always called Paul. At first, his name was Saul, and he was a Pharisee. He was one of the most dedicated Pharisees of all. He did not like Christians because they said Jesus was the Son of God. So he travelled all over Jerusalem and beyond, wherever there were reports about Christians. He wanted to arrest them all and put them to death.

One day, Saul was on his way to Damascus, a city north of Jerusalem. Suddenly a blinding light flashed from heaven and a voice spoke, "Saul, Saul, why do you persecute me?" He fell to the ground and covered his face. He was confused about who was speaking. God? But Saul would never do anything to persecute God.

"Who are you?" he asked.

"I am Jesus, the one you are persecuting."

When Saul uncovered his eyes, he couldn't see. He was blind. His travelling companions had to lead him the rest of the way. Three days later a man visited and healed Saul. His name was Ananias. He laid his hands on Saul and called him "Brother." As soon as he prayed, scales fell from Saul's eyes and he could see again! That day Saul repented and was baptized. He wanted to leave everything about his old self behind so he changed his name to Paul.

But one thing didn't change. Paul still travelled. He travelled even further, on longer trips, and more frequently. Now he travelled out of love for Jesus instead of hatred for Christians. He eventually ended up in the faraway city of Rome, where he was martyred. Paul was one of the busiest missionaries that ever lived, preaching the story of Jesus Christ everywhere he went. He wrote long letters to the churches he established, and these letters became books in the Bible. In the end, Paul wrote more books of the Bible than any other author.

Author's Note

"Faith is confidence in what we hope for and assurance about what we do not see."

HEBREWS 11:1

Hebrews 11, the famous "Hall of Faith," catalogues Old Testament heroes from Abel to King David. The last nine verses begin with an urgent question, "What more shall I say? I do not have time to tell you about Gideon, Barak, Samson, and Jephthah, about David and Samuel and the prophets." But the author then goes on to summarize the rest of the Old Testament in under 250 words.

This passage has always been personal to me. I was twelve when I memorized all nine verses at Bible camp. I found myself coming back to it again and again as I was writing this book. I couldn't include every remarkable person of faith in the Bible, so I used Hebrews 11 as a starting point to decide who to write about. And when I struggled to capture each story on a single page (in about 250 words) I went back to it as inspiration. But most of all I looked to Hebrews 11 as an example of how to teach about faith through story.

What does faith mean, this "confidence in what we hope for," this "assurance" of what we cannot see? How are we supposed to put our faith into practice, if we cannot see what we're believing in? Rather than explain, the author of Hebrews teaches through story. He shows what faith looks like in the lives of Abel, Enoch, Noah, Abraham, and all the rest. Story after story, he brings to life those of whom "the world was not worthy." (Heb. 11:38) Thus, we learn how to live a life of faith and faith's rewards.

My prayer is that the stories in this book provide a similar lesson for you and your family. Here you will find men and women of the Bible, some very familiar to you and others you might be hearing about for the first time, who demonstrated faith in action. I hope that as you read and reread these stories your faith will grow and strengthen, following the example of these faithful friends.

Michael

Artist's Note

I started making dolls for my children. I wanted them to have something fun and whimsical. Something they could toss in the air or cuddle in bed. A soft and snuggly best friend. But I also wanted to make something beautiful, especially when I started making saints and Bible characters. They weren't just dolls but windows into the lives of people of faith—snapshots of holiness. They needed to be easy for little hearts and minds to connect to.

With every doll, I sketch my own patterns. Each design presents a new set of challenges. Like the characters they depict, they have their own personalities. The trick is to uncover it with just the right combination of fabrics. I spent hours poring over each story deciding which elements to display. The fabrics needed to feel authentic and biblical. Warm colors, woven textures, simple patterns and stripes. What would Jesus wear?

Often, I took inspiration from the textiles themselves. Browsing the aisles of fabric bolts, I could see the whole doll as soon as I happened upon the right cloth. Something about a particular color or pattern would strike a chord with me. Since I knew there would be lots of bearded men in a book of Bible characters, I really wanted each one to be unique in the way they dressed.

I have been selling dolls of saints and literary and Bible characters in my online shop Marzipantz for several years. But for this book I wanted to try new things. Instead of flat-lay backgrounds, which I use on social media, I wanted the dolls to have a real sense of place: Miriam dancing with her tambourine, Aaron in his priestly garb, Ruth gleaning Boaz's field, John on the shores of the Sea of Galilee. Each doll needed its own scene, built from cloth. They also needed their own props: a sling, an ark, two stone tablets. I started to feel like a kid again—playing with dolls, dressing them up, putting them in their own stories.

My hope is that all these little details help bring the stories to life so that as you and your children read together you discover not just faithful friends but familiar friends, friends who are close to you, encouraging you in your own life of faith.

Marcy